BRIDGES

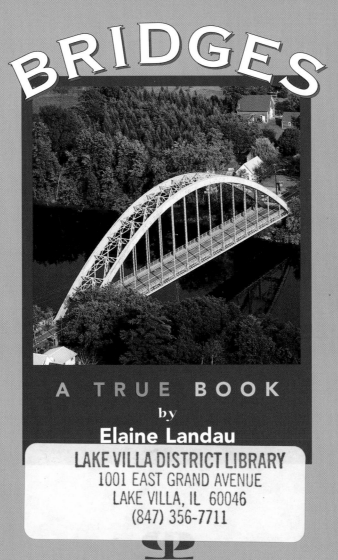

A TRUE BOOK

by

Elaine Landau

Children's Press®
A Division of Scholastic Inc.

New York Toronto London Auckland Sydney
Mexico City New Delhi Hong Kong
Danbury, Connecticut

A horse-drawn carriage enters a covered bridge.

Author's Dedication
For the Great Garmizo
Guys and Girl
Joshua, Jason, and Jessica

Visit Children's Press® on the Internet at:
http://publishing.grolier.com

Library of Congress Cataloging-in-Publication Data

Bridges / by Elaine Landau
    p. cm. — (A true book)
Includes bibliographical references and index.
ISBN 0-516-22182-5 (lib. bdg.)   0-516-27313-2 (pbk.)
    1. Bridges—History—Juvenile literature. 2. Bridges—Design and construction—Juvenile literature. [1. Bridges.] I. Title. II. Series.

TG148 .L36 2001
624'.2—dc21   00-040435

GROLIER
PUBLISHING

Contents

Whether big or small, bridges make our lives easier.

Everyday Marvels

You see bridges everywhere. Big, beautiful bridges are impressive, but the small ones are important too. Bridges allow us to easily cross a lake, a river, or a canyon. Without bridges, some places would be difficult to reach and many journeys would take much longer.

There are many types of bridges. Some bridges are for people to walk across. Others are for cars, trucks, and buses, and there are even special bridges for trains. A bridge can be just a few feet long or span many miles. A modern bridge usually has a framework of concrete, steel, or wood. The roadways, the part we walk or ride across, are generally made of asphalt or concrete.

The Seven Mile Bridge in the Florida Keys (above); Many people drive and walk on the Brooklyn Bridge (right) each day.

Almost every day we have a chance to marvel at these wonderful structures. Bridges help us get where we want to go.

Building Bridges

Today, we have engineers to design our bridges, and we use steel beams and concrete. In the past, people did the best that they could with what they found around them. Early bridges were made of natural materials, such as wood and stone.

This bridge was made from stones.

Whether they are old or new, however, bridges have always been built to be strong. A bridge must be able to withstand all the forces of nature—hurricanes, blizzards, or earthquakes.

These days, engineers build many kinds of bridges. Before they decide which type of bridge to build, they must consider a number of factors. Where will the bridge be built? How will people use the bridge? A bridge designed for people will be narrower than a bridge intended for trains or cars.

A bridge being built in Houston, Texas (above); and an engineer discusses the plans for a bridge with a foreman.

The Bear Mountain Bridge
in New York State

The length of the bridge and the strength, cost, and availability of materials are also extremely important.

In addition, a bridge should fit in well with its surroundings. It should be pleasing to look at. Bridges are structures that communities live with for many years. The best ones are beautiful as well as useful.

Beam Bridges

The beam bridge was probably one of the first types of bridges. To imagine an early beam bridge, just picture a fallen tree. People placed large trees or logs across streams or rivers to cross them. Such bridges were most common in heavily forested areas where

Early beam bridges helped people cross rivers and canyons.

timber was readily available. Some beam bridges were made of several logs tied together and covered with branches. This made them easier—and safer—to cross.

Modern beam bridges are sometimes known as girder bridges. Beams called girders span the needed distance. They are often made of concrete and steel, and used to cross highways. The ends of the girders rest on supports

Girders are placed over supports to build beam bridges.

on each end of the bridge. These supports are called abutments. Extra supports placed at various points

17

The piers on this beam bridge help support it and keep it above the water.

along the girders are called piers. A beam bridge works because the weight of the beam and the load it carries push down on its supports.

Beam bridges are simple in design and cost the least. The most common bridges in the United States today are beam bridges.

A beam bridge raises its draw bridge to let a ship pass through.

Arch Bridges

An arch bridge is shaped like a curve or arch. Simple arch bridges date back thousands of years. The first arch bridges were made of stone. Large stones were wedged together to form an arch that people could walk over. The ancient Romans built many arch

An arch bridge built
by ancient Romans

bridges. Some can still be seen today.

Large modern arch bridges are no longer made of stone though. They are often made of concrete and steel. However, cars or trains could not travel safely over a curved bridge. So the roadway on an arch bridge usually lies either above or below the arch. When the roadway is above the arch it is supported by columns called spandrels. When the roadway

Some arches go above the road . . .
and some go below.

is below the arch, it is supported by beams extending down from the arch.

In an arch bridge, the weight of the bridge and the load it carries are distributed outward along the arch. The supports at both ends of the bridge hold the structure in place. They keep the sides of the bridge from spreading out.

Natchez Trace Bridge

The Natchez Trace Bridge is a famous bridge in Franklin, Tennessee. It has two arches—one is 582 feet

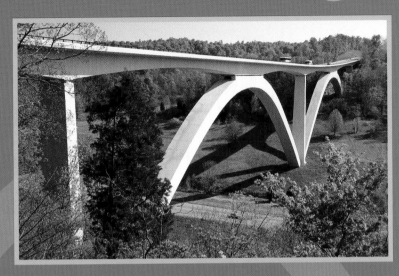

(177 meters) long while the other measures 462 feet (141 m). Together they support the roadway 160 feet (49 m) above the valley floor.

This bridge differs from most arch bridges. Usually when the road is above the arches, it is supported by columns or spandrels. But the Natchez Trace Bridge was built without such supports. Instead, the tops of the arches were somewhat flattened to help them bear the load.

The result is a beautiful bridge with a more open view. Travelers on the Natchez Trace Bridge can fully enjoy the Tennessee scenery.

Suspension Bridges

Like beam bridges and arch bridges, suspension bridges have a long history. The earliest suspension bridges were probably built in tropical areas. Long thick vines as strong as rope were plentiful there. They were the basic building materials for the first suspension bridges.

The Benjamin Franklin Bridge in Philadelphia, Pennsylvania

A suspension bridge
made from vines

The vines were tied to trees or boulders on each side of a lake or canyon. Additional vines were tied several feet higher. As people crossed the bridge, they held on to the higher vines while stepping on the lower ones. These early suspension bridges must have swayed in the wind, but people usually made it to the other side.

Modern suspension bridges are based on this

idea but are much more secure. In today's bridges, the roadway is suspended, or hung, from huge wire cables. The cables, which are attached to the tops of high towers, stretch from one end of the bridge to the other. Both ends of the cable are firmly anchored in huge concrete blocks. In a suspension bridge, most of the bridge's weight is distributed through the cables to the anchored points.

From above, you can see how the cables help support the bridge.

There are many suspension bridges across the country, including this one in New York City.

Suspension bridges can span a greater distance than any other bridge. This is partly because the cables may extend far away from the towers. Some people think these bridges are the most beautiful. However, they are also the most costly to build. Nevertheless, these impressive bridges are extremely popular in the United States. More of them are built here than anywhere else in the world.

The Golden Gate Bridge

California's Golden Gate Bridge connects San Francisco to northern California. At first some people thought this suspension bridge would never be built. Engineers and construction crews had to deal with extremely difficult weather conditions. Heavy fog and high winds are common there. And powerful ocean currents flow through the canyon at that

point. Yet, after four years of hard work, the bridge was completed in 1937. Unfortunately, eleven people were killed during its construction.

The Golden Gate Bridge spans 8,981 feet (2,737 m) and cost more than $35 million to construct. You might be surprised to learn that the bridge was painted orange. That color was chosen because it blended in with the area's natural environment. Cars and trucks travel on this marvelous bridge every day. Special pathways are provided for bikers and pedestrians.

Bridging a Community

Sometimes a bridge does more than help people get from place to place. A good example is the Community Bridge in Frederick, Maryland, not far from Washington, D.C. Here, the local community worked together to transform a bridge into a work of art.

It looks like an arch bridge, but it's really a beam bridge!

First, in a project known as Bridge Builders Outreach, people from near and far were asked an important question. They had to name an object that represents the true spirit of community to them. One teenager answered: "Two hands—one black and one white—one helping the other over the wall." This image, along with many others, appears on the Community Bridge.

One of the many designs
on the Community Bridge

Discover for Yourself

Bridges are all around us. Your town or city probably has at least one. You may cross a bridge to get to school. Or perhaps you travel over several bridges when you visit a particular friend or relative.

The next time you see a bridge—look at it carefully. Is it a suspension bridge, or an arch bridge, or a beam bridge? You know what to look for now. Examine the bridge to see if it has any special features. If you were an engineer, how would you have designed it? Would you have done anything differently?

You might want to do some sketches of imaginary

Can you name the types of bridges on these two pages?

bridges—bridges you wish
existed. Try drawing your
dream bridge. Someday you
may be building it.

To Find Out More

Here are some additional resources to help you learn more about bridges:

 **Books**

Carter, Polly. **The Bridge Book.** Simon & Schuster, 1992.

Cooper, Jason. **Bridges.** Rourke, 1991.

Dunn, Andrew. **Bridges.** Thomson Learning, 1993.

Gaff, Jackie. **Buildings, Bridges, & Tunnels.** Random House, 1991.

Hill, Lee Sullivan. **Bridges Connect.** Carolrhoda Books, 1997.

Oxlade, Chris. **Bridges.** Raintree Steck-Vaughn, 1997.

Richardson, Joy. **Bridges.** Franklin Watts, 1994.

Robbins, Ken. **Bridges.** Dial Books, 1991.

Royston, Angela. **Buildings, Bridges, and Tunnels.** Warwick Press, 1991.

Sturges, Philemon. **Bridges Are to Cross.** G. P. Putnam's Sons, 1998.

💡 Organizations and Online Sites

Brooklyn Bridge
*http://brooklynjuniorleague.
org/BRIDGE.HTM*

Read a short history of the
Brooklyn Bridge with links
to interesting photographs.

**Buildings, Bridges,
and Tunnels**
*http://www.discovery.com/
stories/technology/
buildings/bridges.html*

Learn about the longest
suspension bridge and
explore bridges around
the world.

Covered Bridges of Maine
*http://www.state.me.us/
mdot/maint_op/covered/
coverbrg.htm*

View pictures and maps of
Maine's covered bridges
and read about their history.

London Bridge
*http://www.towerbridge.
org.uk/*

Discover London's Tower
Bridge—one of the world's
most famous bridges.

Super Bridge
*http://www.pbs.org/wgbh/
nova/bridge/*

Build your own bridge
online, and learn more
about the different types
of bridges.

Important Words

abutments supports on each end of a beam bridge

asphalt a sticky, dark material used for paving roads

girder a type of heavy beam

piers structures that help support a bridge

roadway the surface cars drive on

spandrels columns that support an arch bridge

Index

Meet the Author

Award-winning author Elaine Landau worked as a newspaper reporter, an editor, and a youth services librarian before becoming a full-time writer. She has written more than one hundred and fifty nonfiction books for young people, including True Books on dinosaurs, animals, countries, and food.

Ms. Landau, who has a bachelor's degree in English and journalism from New York University and a master's degree in library and information science from Pratt Institute, lives in Florida with her husband and son.